Music for Little People

50 Playful Activities for Preschool and Early Elementary School Children

Compiled by
John M. Feierabend

Illustrated by
Gary M. Kramer

BOOSEY & HAWKES

CONTENTS

MOVING FINGERS

—Use piano when teach song

MOVING BODIES

MOVING TOGETHER

MOVING AROUND

MOVING VOICES

TAKING TURNS

LEADING OTHERS

ACKNOWLEDGEMENTS

Special thanks to Ann C. Kay as well as Mary Beth Ming and her students at the Shepard Boulevard Elementary School in Columbia, Missouri who shared songs that appear in this book. Recognition is here expressed to Andrea Macon and the Children's Chorus of Maryland for participating in the production of the accompanying cassette. Appreciation is also expressed to Sr. Lorna Zemke and Edwin Gordon who enhanced my teaching and my understanding of how children learn. Finally and most importantly I am indebted to my own children Andrew, Charles, and James who have shown me that if given the chance, music can become essential in children's lives far beyond anything I ever thought I was teaching in a music class.

John M. Feierabend   Ph.D.
Collector and Author
Father of three "Little People"
Professor of Music Education
Early Childhood Music Specialist

Gary M. Kramer
Illustrator
Father of two "Little People"
Director, Video Resources Studio
Studio Artist

Luann Saunders
Vocals and Guitar
Mother of two "Little People"
Music Educator
Folksinger

For James and Geoffrey

INTRODUCTION

As children develop from toddlers to preschoolers (around 30 months) their interest in music making becomes more evident. Preschool children love to make music, repeating fragments of familiar songs and developing their own songs. The richer a child's exposure to songs and rhymes, the more imaginative his spontaneous song making can become.

Songs and rhymes in early childhood can be a playful way of enhancing essential developmental skills. They teach concepts, enhance vocabulary, they develop motor skills, and encourage social skills and creative responses. They are happy experiences for children.

Traditional songs and rhymes were selected for this collection for many reasons. They are not contrived. They are singable by young children. They are a natural union of words, rhythm, and melody. They were created by ordinary people out of inspiration. They are living examples of our cultural past. They contain and transmit real human feeling. They are our native musical language. They belong to us.

The other consideration for assembling this collection was to provide activities which would enhance children's abilities to be successful with making music. The path to language ability in early childhood is listening, understanding and the coordination ability necessary to express one's self which progresses from babbling to precision. Music making ability follows a similar course. The motor coordination and vocal coordination necessary to perform songs and rhymes also progresses from "babbling'" to precision.

Songs and rhymes which require less rhythmic precision and are not performed with a consistent pulse are found in "Moving Fingers" and "Moving Bodies". Those activities which encourage the precision of a consistent pulse are in "Moving Together", "Moving Around", and "Leading Others". Awareness of potential vocal ability is the focus of "Moving Voices", while songs which encourage the development of vocal precision are included in "Taking Turns".

TXB-70   Printed in U.S.A.

MOVING FINGERS

The following songs and rhymes include movements which pretend the actions of the words. These activities can be performed while sitting since you will only be using the upper part of your body. When sharing these activities, learn the movements that will be used before you learn the song or the rhyme. If you first learn the movements and then the song or rhyme, you will be better able to combine them. Ready? Can you make your fingers look like this?

1 Help Me Wind My Ball of Wool

Help me wind my ball of wool.

Hold it gen - tly; Do not pull,

Wind the wool and wind the wool, A -

round, a - round, a - round.

or

or

or

2 Chop, Chop, Chippity Chop

Chop, chop, chip-pi-ty chop, cut off the bot-tom and cut off the top.

What we have left we'll put in the pot; chop, chop, chip-pi-ty chop!

Chop, chop,

cut off the bottom

cut off the top.

What we have left

we'll put in the pot;

chop, chop,

3 Grandma's Glasses

Grandma's glasses,

These are Grand-ma's glass-es, And

this is Grand-ma's hat, And

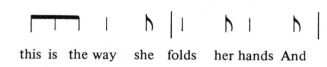

this is the way she folds her hands And

lays them in her lap.

hat

folds her hands

lays them in her lap.

Grandpa's glasses.

hat

folds his arms

Verse 2.

These are Grandpa's glasses,
And this is Grandpa's hat,
And this is the way he folds his arms
Just like that.

Just like that.

4 Do Your Ears Hang Low?

Do your ears hang low? Do they
wob-ble to and fro? Can you
tie them in a knot? Can you
tie them in a bow? Can you
throw them o-ver your shoul-der Like a
con-ti-nen-tal sol-dier? Do your
ears hang low?

ears hang low?

wobble to and fro?

tie them in a knot?

tie them in a bow?

over your shoulder

continental soldier?

ears hang low?

11

5 Five Little Ladies

Five lit-tle la-dies go-ing for a walk.

Five lit-tle la-dies stop-ping for a talk. A-

long came five lit-tle gen-tle-men, They

all danced to-geth-er and then there were ten.

going for a walk.

stopping for a talk.

five little gentlemen,

all danced together

6 Eensy Weensy Spider

The een-sy ween-sy spi-der climbed
up the wa-ter spout.
Down came the rain and
washed the spi-der out.
Out came the sun and
dried up all the rain, And the
een-sy ween-sy spi-der climbed
up the spout a gain.

eensy weensy spider   alternate   up the water spout.   Down came   washed the spider out.

Out came   dried up all the rain,   eensy weensy spider   alternate   up the spout again.

Verse 2:   The eensy weensy spider kept climbing up the spout.
He climbed and he climbed while trying to get out;
He kept right on climbing and never did he stop.
And the eensy weensy spider, at last he reached the top.

14

7 Three Little Monkeys

jumping on the bed,

One fell off

bumped his head,

called the doctor,

No more monkeys

Verse 2.   Two little monkeys . . .
          (use two fingers)

Verse 3.   One little monkey . . .
          (use one finger)

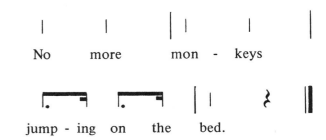

Three   lit - tle   mon - keys

jump - ing   on   the   bed,

One   fell   off   and

bumped   his   head,

Ma - ma called the   doc - tor,   the

doc - tor   said,

No   more   mon - keys

jump - ing   on   the   bed.

15

8 Miss Polly Had a Dolly

Miss Pol-ly had a dol-ly who was sick, sick, sick. She

phoned for the doc-tor to come quick, quick, quick. The

doc-tor came with his bag and his hat. He

knocked on the door with a rat a tat tat. He

looked at the dol-ly and he shook his head. He

said, "Miss Pol-ly, put her straight to bed." He

wrote on a pa-per for a pill, pill, pill. "I'll be

back in the morn-ing with the bill, bill, bill."

Miss Polly had a dolly

phoned for the doctor

doctor came

knocked on the door

shook his head.

put her straight to bed

wrote on a paper

back in the morning

16

9 Mr. Lynn

Mis - ter Lynn is ver - y thin, Mis - ter Pratt is ver - y fat,

Mis - ter Cort is ver - y short, Mis - ter Hall is ver - y tall,

Mis - ter Dent is ver - y bent, Mis - ter Wait is ver - y straight.

very thin,

very fat,

very short,

very tall,

very bent,

very straight.

10 Five Little Mice

Five lit - tle mice came out to play Gath - er - ing crumbs a - long the way. Out came the pus - sy - cat sleek and fat. Four lit - tle mice went scamp - er - ing back.

ONE HAND

Five little mice

and fat.

THE OTHER HAND

Out the came the pussy cat

went scampering back.

Start with hands behind your back. Repeat the rhyme, each time with one less finger until "No little mice went scampering back."

MOVING BODIES

You will need to be ready to stand up and sit down and maybe stand up again with the following songs and rhymes. We will be moving our whole bodies as we act out the motions of the words. As with the previous section you should learn the movements for each song or rhyme before you add the words and music. Gather your energy. Here we go!

11 The Jack-in-the-Box

The jack-in-the-box jumps up. The
jack-in-the-box goes flop. The
jack-in-the-box goes a-round and a-round, And the
lid comes down with a plop!

jumps up.

goes flop.

around and around,

down with a plop!

12 Wake Up You Lazy Bones

Wake up

cows are gone.

sun is hot.

I'll rest

'till they come home.

D

Wake up you la - zy bones and

A7 D

go and fetch the cat - tle.

Wake up you la - zy bones and

A7 D *Fine*

go and fetch the cows.

A7 D

The cows are gone.

A7 D

The sun is hot.

A7 D

I think I'll rest

A7 *D. C. al Fine* D

'till they come home.

Shout: "Wake up you lazy bones."

13 Cousin Peter

Action Song

Last — eve - ning cous - in — Pe - ter came,

Last — eve - ning cous - in — Pe - ter came,

Last — eve - ning cous - in — Pe - ter came

Just to say that he was here.

Verse 2: He wiped his feet upon the mat (3 times)
Just to show that he was here.

Verse 3: He hung his hat upon the peg (3 times)
Just to show that he was here.

Verse 4: He played he was a great big bear (3 times)
Just to show that he was here.

Verse 5: He picked me up into the air (3 times)
Just to show that he was here.

Verse 6: He made a bow and said said "Goodbye" (3 times)
Just to show that he was here.

cousin Peter came,

wiped his feet

hung his hat

great big bear

picked me up

made a bow

alternate

said "Goodbye"

14 Head and Shoulders, Knees and Toes

Head and shoul-ders, knees and toes, knees and toes, Head and shoul-ders, knees and toes, knees and toes,— My —

eyes and ears and mouth — and — nose, Head and shoul-ders, knees and toes, knees and toes.

Head

shoulders,

knees

toes,

eyes

ears

mouth

nose,

15 The Wheels on the Bus

F

The wheels on the bus go round and round,

C7   **F**

Round and round, round and round, The

wheels on the bus go round and round,

C7   **F**

All day long.

wheels   horn   wipers   driver

people   baby   mother

Verse 2.   The horn on the bus goes peep, peep, peep . . .

Verse 3.   The wipers on the bus go swish, swish, swish . . .

Verse 4.   The driver on the bus says, "Move on back," . . .

Verse 5.   The people on the bus bounce up and down . . .

Verse 6.   The baby on the bus says, "Wah, wah, wah," . . .

Verse 7.   The mother on the bus says, "Sh, sh, sh," . . .

16 The Noble Duke of York

noble Duke

ten thousand men,

top of the hill,

down again;

up

down

halfway up

of York

ten thousand men,

Oh, the no-ble Duke of York, He

had ten thou-sand men, He

marched them up to the top of the hill, And he

marched them down a - gain; Oh, and

when you're up you're up; And

when you're down you're down; And

when you're on - ly half-way up you're

half - way to the ground.

17 What the Animals Do

We'll hop, hop, hop like a bun-ny, And
run, run, run like a dog; We'll
walk, walk, walk like an e-le-phant, And
jump, jump, jump like a frog. We'll

hop,

run,

walk,

swim, swim, swim like a gold-fish, And
fly, fly, fly like a bird; We'll
sit right down and fold our hands and say
not a sin-gle word.

jump,

swim,

fly,

sit right down

say not a single word.

29

18 The Wiggle Song

My thumbs are start-ing to wig - gle, My
thumbs are start - ing to wig - gle, My
thumbs are start - ing to wig - gle, A -
round, a - round, a - round.

Verse 2: My thumbs and fingers are wiggling . . .

Verse 3: My hands are starting to wiggle . . .

Verse 4: My arms are starting to wiggle . . .

Verse 5: My head is starting to wiggle . . .

Verse 6: My legs are starting to wiggle . . .

Verse 7: Now all of me is awiggle . . .

thumbs are starting
(Add additional body parts with each verse)

all of me is awiggle

MOVING TOGETHER

Sometimes we can maintain a consistant pulse as we perform some movement with a song or a rhyme. Even though we will be moving by ourselves we will be moving at the same time as each other. Repeat each motion keeping a consistant pulse from the beginning of the song until the end. Can we do our movements together?

19 I Can Hammer

I can ham-mer with one ham - mer,

I can ham-mer with one ham - mer,

I can ham-mer with one ham - mer, And

ham-mer and ham-mer all day.

Verse 2: I can hammer with two hammers . . .

Verse 3: I can hammer with three hammers . . .

Verse 4: I can hammer with four hammers . .

Verse 5: I can hammer with five hammers . . .

one hammer,

two hammers

three hammers

four hammers

five hammers

or

five hammers

20 Haul Away Joe!

Way, haul a - way, ____ Oh

haul and sing to - geth - er. ____

Way, haul a - way. ____ We'll

haul a - way Joe!

21 One Finger, One Thumb

One finger,
one thumb,

and

chase the
flies away.

One fin-ger, one thumb, keep mov - ing, keep

mov - ing, keep mov - ing, One

fin - ger, one thumb, keep mov - ing And

chase the flies a - way.

Verse 2: Two fingers, two thumbs, keep moving . . .

Verse 3: Two fingers, two thumbs, two arms, keep moving . . .

Verse 4: Two fingers, two thumbs, two arms, two feet, keep moving . . .

Verse 5: Two fingers, two thumbs, two arms, two feet, stand up, sit down, keep moving . . .

*Extra words inserted here are sung on the same tone as "one thumb".

Two fingers, two thumbs,

Two fingers, two thumbs, two arms,

Two fingers, two thumbs, two arms, two feet,

stand up, sit down,

22 The Horse Stood Around

Oh, the horse stood a-round with his foot on the ground, Oh, the

horse stood a - round with his foot on the ground, Oh, the

horse stood a - round with his foot on the ground, Oh, the

horse stood a - round — with his foot on the ground.

Verse 2. *(spoken before repeat)*

Same horse, the o-ther foot.

Verse 3. *(spoken before repeat)*

Same horse, chang-ing feet.

Verse 4. *(spoken before repeat)*

Same horse, both feet.

Verse 5. *(spoken before repeat)*

Same horse, one foot.

horse stood around

the other foot.

changing feet.

both feet.

one foot.

37

23 Ali Baba and the Forty Thieves

Leader chants and performs a motion on the beat. Children repeat chant and motion.

Al - i   Ba - ba and the for - ty thieves

 or or

Possible motions to perform on the beat with chant.

tap legs
tap floor
clap hands
tap head
nod head
touch nose
pull ears
snap fingers

Later:

Leader performs the chant and first motion. While children are repeating the chant with the first motion, the leader is simultaneously performing a second motion. While the children are performing the chant with the second motion, the leader is simultaneously performing a third motion . . . etc. . . . .

Later:

Children sit in a circle, leader performs the first motion. While the first child echos the chant and first motion, the leader is simultaneously performing a second motion. Next, the second child echos the first motion, the first child simultaneously echos the second motion, and the leader simultaneously performs a third motion. This chain is continued until all children are performing different motions simultaneously.

24 Mother Goonie Bird

"Right wing"

"Left wing"

"Right foot"

"Left foot"

"Now your head"

"Sit down"

Verse 2. *"Left wing"*
Verse 3. *"Right foot"*
Verse 4. *"Left foot"*
Verse 5. *"Now your head"*
Verse 6. *"Sit down"*

Motion:

1. Moth-er Goon-ie Bird had sev-en chicks, sev-en chicks had Moth-er Goon-ie Bird, And they could-n't walk, And they could-n't talk, But they could all go like this. *"Right wing"*

© Copyright John M. Feierabend 1986.

40

25 See How I'm Jumping

See how I'm jump-ing, jump-ing, jump-ing!

See how I'm bounc-ing like a ball.

You did-n't know I could jump so high.

You did-n't know I could stand so still.

See how I'm jump-ing, jump-ing, jump-ing.

When I am tir-ed down I flop.

See how I'm jumping, stand so still. See how I'm jumping, down I flop.

41

MOVING AROUND

Some songs need the help of a few friends. You might find yourself holding hands in a line or sitting in a circle. Together, you will be asked to move or move something around. Move with the same pulse as everyone else and see how much fun moving around can be.

26 Alley–Alley–O

Oh the big ship sail-ing on the al-ley al-ley-o, The al-ley-al-ley-o, The al-ley-al-ley-o; Oh the big ship sail-ing on the al-ley-al-ley-o; On the nine-teenth of Sep-tem-ber.

27 Slip One and Two

Slip one and two,
jump three and four,
Turn a-round quick-ly and
sit up-on the floor.
Clap one and two,
nod three and four,
Jump up a-gain and be
read-y for more.

Slip one and two,

jump

Turn around quickly

sit upon the floor.

Clap

nod

Jump up again and
be ready for more.

28 Wind the Bobbin

Wind the bobbin,

F

NO

Wind the bob-bin, Ding Dong. Gon-na

Wind it tight, Ding Dong.

Bob-bin a wound up, Bob-bin a wound up,

Bob-bin a wound up. Ding Dong. Gon-na
Last verse: "Break it."

"Break it."

29 Hey Betty Martin

Chorus: (F) Hey Bet-ty Mar-tin, tip-py toe, tip-py toe, (C7) Hey Bet-ty Mar-tin tip-toe fine. (F) Hey Bet-ty Mar-tin, tip-py toe, tip-py toe, (C7) Hey Bet-ty Mar-tin (F) tip-toe fine. *Fine*

Verse: (C7) Jump with me, I'll (F) jump with you; (C7) We'll go jump-ing the (F) whole day through. (C7) Jump so fine, jump (F) so fine, (G7) Jump-ing, jump-ing (C) all the time. *D. C. al Fine*

tippy toe,

Jump with me,   or

30 Pass the Shoe

I pass the shoe from me to you, to you, I
pass the shoe and this is what I do.

Early: While group sits on the floor in a circle, pass the shoe.
Each individual should set the shoe down on the beat,
in front of the person sitting next to him.

Later: While group sits on the floor in a circle, each child re-
moves one shoe. All children pass a shoe on each beat.

** Try passing other objects such as a cup (paper or styrofoam), bean bag, or stuffed animal.
* Pass.

10 Five Little Mice

$\frac{6}{8}$

Five lit - tle mice came out to play Gath - er - ing

crumbs a - long the way. Out came the pus - sy - cat sleek and

fat. Four lit - tle mice went scamp - er - ing back.

ONE HAND

Five little mice

and fat.

THE OTHER HAND

Out the came the pussy cat

went scampering back.

Start with hands behind your back. Repeat the rhyme, each time with one less finger until "No little mice went scampering back."

19

16 The Noble Duke of York

noble Duke

ten thousand men,

top of the hill,

down again;

up

down

D.C.

halfway up

of York

ten thousand men,

Oh, the no-ble Duke of York, He

D7
had ten thou-sand men, He

G **C**
marched them up to the top of the hill, And he

G **D7** **G** *Fine*
marched them down a-gain; Oh, and

when you're up you're up; And

D7
when you're down you're down; And

G **C**
when you're on-ly half-way up you're

G **D7** **G** *D.C. al Fine*
half-way to the ground.

41 Down by the Bay

Leader: **G**   Echo:

Down   by   the   bay, Down   by   the   bay,

D7

Where the wa-ter-me-lons grow, Where the wa-ter-mel-ons grow,

Back   to   my   home, Back   to   my   home,

G

I   dare   not   go,   I   dare   not   go,

C

For   if   I   do, For   if   I   do,

G

My   moth-er will   say, My   moth-er will   say,

Leader or Solo:

Verse 1. "Did   you   ev - er   see   a   bear

All sing:
D7   **G**

comb-ing   his   hair?"   Down   by   the   bay.

Down by the bay,

Down by the bay,

"Did you ever see

2. "Did you ever see a bee
   With a sunburned knee?" . . .

3. "Did you ever see a moose
   Kissing a goose?" . . .

4. "Did you ever see a whale
   With a polkadot tail?" . . .

5. "Did you ever see a fly
   Wearing a tie?" . . .

65

42 Oh, You Can't Get to Heaven

Leader: F   Echo:

1. Oh, you can't get to heav-en, Oh you can't get to heav-en,

B♭   F   B♭   F

On a pair of skates, __ On a pair of skates, __

C7

You'll skate right by, You'll skate right by,

F   C7   F

Those pearl-y gates, __ Those pearl-y gates, __

All sing: B♭

Oh, you can't get to heav-en on a pair of skates, You'll skate right

F   C7

by those pearl-y gates, Oh, I ain't a-gon-na grieve my Lord no

F   B♭

more, Oh I ain't a gon-na grieve my Lord no more, Oh I ain't a gon-na

F   C7   F

grieve my Lord no more, Oh I ain't a gon-na grieve my Lord no more. __

2. Oh, you can't get to heaven*
   In a rocking chair . . .
   'Cause the Lord don't want . . .
   No lazy bones there . . .

All: Oh you can't get to heaven in a rocking chair,
'Cause the Lord don't want no lazy bones there,
Oh I ain't a gonna grieve my Lord no more.
Oh I ain't a gonna grieve my Lord no more,
Oh I ain't a gonna grieve my Lord no more,
Oh I ain't a gonna grieve my Lord no more.

3. Oh, you can't get to heaven . . .
   In a limousine . . .
   'Cause the Lord don't sell . . .
   No gasoline . . .

All: Oh, you can't get to heaven . . . (etc.)

4. Oh, you can't get to heaven . . .
   In a motor car . . .
   'Cause a motor car . . .
   Won't go that far . . .

All: Oh, you can't get to heaven . . . (etc.)

5. Oh, you can't get to heaven . . .
   In a birch canoe . . .
   You'll need to paddle . . .
   'Till you're black and blue . . .

All: Oh, you can't get to heaven . . . (etc.)

6. If you get to heaven . . .
   Before I do . . .
   Just bore a hole . . .
   And pull me through . . .

All: If you get to heaven . . . (etc.)

*Echo each phrase.

Oh, you can't get

Oh, you can't get

(All sing)

LEADING OTHERS

Most of us enjoy becoming a leader once in a while. Here are some songs in which we will take turns leading each other with our favorite repeated movement. Make sure your repeated movement has a consistant pulse so it will be easy to follow. When following another leader imitate his movement and his pulse. Ready? Do this.

43 Dame Get Up

Dame get up— and bake your pies,

Bake your pies, Bake your pies,

Dame get up— and bake your pies on

this fine day in the morn - ing.

or

44 Puncinella

G

Now look who is here, Pun - ci - nel - la, Pun - ci - nel - la,

D7   G

Look who is here, Pun - ci - nel - la in the shoe.

look who is here,

what can you do   or

Verse 2. Now what can you do
Puncinella, Puncinella . . .

Verse 3. Now we can do it too
Puncinella, Puncinella . . .

Verse 4. Now who do you choose
Puncinella, Puncinella . . .

we can do it too

who do you choose

70

45 The Monkey Stomps

The mon-key stomps, stomps, stomps his feet, The
mon-key stomps, stomps, stomps his feet.
Mon-key see; mon-key do; The
mon-key does the same as you.

46 Francisco

1. Take off your shoes and stock-ings And if your feet go bare, ___ Fran C - I - S - CO, C - I - S - CO, Shake it if you care, Oh,

2. Shake it baby, shake it.
   Shake it if you care.
   Fran - C - I - S - CO, C - I - S - CO.
   Shake it if you care, Oh!

3. Tumble to the bottom,
   Tumble to the top.
   Turn yourself around and around
   And then you have to STOP!

Take off your shoes and stockings

Shake it baby,

or

Tumble to the bottom,

47 My Mother Sent Me Unto You

My moth-er sent me un-to you. What to do? What to do? My moth-er sent me

un - to you, To do — with one as I do, To do — with one as I do.

+ pg 50
Old King Glory
Fma

or

48 Dayenu

We are marching out of E-gypt, Fol-low-ing our no-ble lead-er,

March-ing proud-ly, sing-ing loud-ly, Da-ye-nu. Da-da-ye-nu,—

Da-da-ye-nu,— Da-da-ye-nu, Da-ye-nu, Da-ye-nu.

We are marching

Da - da - ye - nu,

or

49 William Had Seven Sons

Dm

Wil-liam had — sev - en sons, sev - en sons, sev - en sons,

Gm   Dm

A7   Dm

Wil-liam had — sev - en sons and this is what they did.

or

or

77

50 Ambos a Dos

Ambos a dos,

What will you do,

Now we can do it too,

or

Am - bos a dos, ma-ta - ri - le, ri - le, ri - le, Am -

bos a dos, ma - ta - ri - le, ri - le, ron.

Now who do you choose,

2. What will you do, matarile, rile, rile,
   What will you do, matarile, rile, ron?

3. Now we can do it too, matarile, rile, rile,
   Now we can do it too, matarile, rile, ron.

4. Now who do you choose, matarile, rile, rile,
   Now who do you choose, matarile, rile, ron?

ALPHABETICAL LISTING

SUBJECT INDEX

ABOUT ME AND MY BODY

ABOUT OTHER PEOPLE

ABOUT OTHER LIVING THINGS

ABOUT THINGS TO EAT

ABOUT GETTING THERE